The Memoirs of Andrew Sherburne

The Memoirs of

ANDREW SHERBURNE

Patriot and Privateer
of the American Revolution

Edited by Karen Zeinert

Illustrated by Seymour Fleishman

LINNET BOOKS 1993

JUVENILE
BIOGRAPHY
Sherburne,

A

Library of Congress Cataloging-in-Publication Data

Sherburne, Andrew, 1765–1831
The memoirs of Andrew Sherburne,
patriot and privateer of the American Revolution
edited by Karen Zeinert; illustrated by Seymour Fleishman
p.   cm.
Includes bibliographical references.
Summary: Excerpts from the author's autobiography
recall his experiences as a thirteen-year-old boy
serving on an American privateer ship
during the Revolutionary War.
1. Sherburne, Andrew, 1765–1831—Juvenile literature.
2. United States—History—Revolution, 1775–1783—Personal
narratives—Juvenile literature.
3. United States—History—Revolution, 1775–1783—Naval
operations—Juvenile literature.   4. Privateering—United
States—History—18th century—Juvenile literature.
5. Seamen—United States—Biography—Juvenile literature.
[1. Sherburne, Andrew, 1765–1831.   2. United States—
History—Revolution, 1775–1783—Personal narratives.
3. Privateering.   4. Seamen.]
I. Fleishman, Seymour, ill.   II. Title.
E271.S54   1993   973'5—dc20   92-20542
ISBN 0-208-02354-2

Printed in the United States of America

CONTENTS

INTRODUCTION

In 1779, thirteen-year-old Andrew Sherburne joined America's new navy. This navy had been started by the Continental Congress shortly after the Revolutionary War began in 1775. Needing ships quickly for the war effort and having none, Congress started to build its navy by buying boats from merchants wherever it could. It armed these ships with guns seized from British supply depots in the colonies.

But few vessels were available, so Congress then asked colonial shipyards, such as those in Portsmouth, New Hampshire, Andrew's home town, to build men-o-war instead of fishing boats. The new ships were put under the command of military men with some sailing experience, and the officers recruited and trained would-be sailors.

The new navy had four duties. First, it was supposed to stop British soldiers from getting to the colonies by capturing British ships bringing troops to America. Second, since Washington's men were in desperate need of guns and bullets, and the British had plenty of both, the navy was expected to capture as many arms shipments as possible. Not only would this hurt the enemy, it would arm Washington's men quickly and cheaply. Third, the navy was supposed to protect merchantmen, trading vessels, on the Atlantic Ocean, and fourth, it was authorized to capture English merchantmen.

Some of the most valuable trade at that time was conducted between the colonists and islands in the West Indies, such as Jamaica. Colonists shipped grain, fish, horses, and wooden barrels to the islands to be sold, and Yankee ships returned loaded with sugar, molasses (which was used to make rum), silver, and even gold. Also, colonists sold meat, fish, lumber, and grain to European markets, and they exchanged rum in Africa for slaves. At the same time, the British were buying fish from Newfoundland, one of their Canadian colonies, and sugar and molasses from the West Indies. In short, many ships loaded with goods worth a fortune were sailing on the ocean regularly, and both the English and the Americans used their navies to protect some of these vessels.

Life aboard Continental ships was regulated by the head of the navy. Captains earned $32 a month, and boys like Andrew received $6.66 for thirty days of work. Food was handed out once each day, and sailors ate whenever they wished, often cooking—and eating—their meals with the same group of men, known as their messmates. Sailors received one pound of bread daily plus a pound of pork or beef and one of three vegetables—a pound of potatoes, turnips, or half a pound of peas. Butter was available once a week, and cheese was distributed on Mondays, Thursdays, and Saturdays.

In those days, sailors could enlist for short periods of time. But this meant that men were coming and going regularly, so they were responsible for getting to and from their ships on their own.

Also, it was not uncommon to have twenty or more boys twelve, thirteen, and fourteen years old as part of a ship's crew. Children at that time were expected to work at a young age. Colonial families were often large, and older children had to help with household chores and care for younger brothers and sisters. If a family owned a business or a farm, children worked in the shop or in the fields for many hours at a time as soon as they were able to do so. During the war, many boys were more than willing to volunteer to go to sea to escape their routine at home. They knew they'd earn some money, and they hoped to find adventure as well.

But Congress lacked money, and it couldn't possibly buy enough ships or hire enough sailors to make a powerful navy. To help the cause, Congress offered letters of marque and reprisal, documents that gave permission to individuals, who were called privateers, to attack and seize British ships. If caught by the enemy, privateers could show their letters and expect to be treated as prisoners of war. But these documents didn't always protect them. Sometimes the enemy regarded privateers as nothing more than pirates, and they were shot or hanged when caught.

Almost 1,700 colonial privateer ships sailed at some time between 1775 and 1781. Their crews seized ships, goods, and arms and munitions worth millions of dollars. Some sources estimate the total take for seven years at

$24,000,000 while others believe it ran as high as $50,000,000. In either case, it was a lot of money. Captured ships, prizes, were usually taken to the closest friendly port. Cargoes were sold there, and the profits were divided among the privateers—just as they were on the navy's ships—according to a prearranged formula. The ship's captain or captains got the most goods. ("Captain" was often an honorary title then, and more than one captain could be found on a ship, especially on privateers.) The newest hand on deck received the least. Seaworthy prizes were manned, renamed, and sent out to catch more enemy ships.

While privateering helped the patriots' cause, it also made people rich. Even some of the newest hands received $1,000 on a successful voyage. Captains in the navy didn't earn that much in a whole year, and no soldier in General Washington's army—and few civilians—could ever expect to receive that sum in such a short period of time. Therefore, even though privateering was dangerous, it attracted many colonists. By the end of the war, almost 60,000 Americans had been at sea looking for enemy ships.

In the beginning of the war, privateering was relatively easy. The British, knowing that the Americans had no navy, took few precautions to protect their ships. Many vessels were armed lightly, and merchantmen had no arms at all, often sailing without armed escorts to protect them. However, once privateering began and the British armed as many ships as possible, trying to capture English ships became a risky business.

Although privateering was no better than piracy to some people, it was held in high esteem by many colonists. Before the war, England had decided what products could be sent to the colonies, and the English parliament had placed high taxes on most of them, which made them very expensive. During the war, privateers supplied merchants with inexpensive products that had not been available previously. Colonists eagerly bought up these bargains, and businesses thrived, making customers and merchants very happy.

Also, the colonists were well aware that without the help of privateers, equipment and weapons needed to fight the war would not have been available. They knew that if the British could control the seas, they could simply wait for the colonists to run out of supplies. This would have eventually forced the Americans to surrender. So because privateering helped the patriots' cause, it had the solid support of government leaders as well as anyone who wanted to be free of British rule.

The British navy may have seemed very powerful to the colonists, but it had a serious weakness. Although it had many vessels, it couldn't find enough sailors to man its ships during the war. The British government had little money with which to pay its sailors—it hadn't raised salaries in over one hundred years!—and few men were willing to go to sea as long as there were other ways to earn a living.

To complete crews, the British government authorized its navy to capture, or impress, men to work on ships. Some British sailors were organized into small groups called press gangs. These gangs went on shore while their ship was in port, looking for able-bodied seamen. In some cases, guard ships dropped anchor in English ports for long periods of time, and they captured men daily, holding them on board until an English captain requested sailors for his ship.

To prevent impressed men from escaping, vessels were anchored far from shore in all ports. Transport boats, small boats used for errands between ship and shore, were guarded carefully. Once a man was on board, it was not unusual for him to serve for many years.

British captains could release men any time they wished, though. Sometimes men were promised—and given—freedom after a certain time if they worked hard. This tended to make them cooperative.

Although most impressed sailors came from the British Isles, American colonists were captured for the king's service, too. Americans hated impressment, and they fought back by mobbing press gangs and burning their boats. Citizens of Boston actually rioted in 1747 when press gangs appeared in their city and began to drag Americans away.

The Revolutionary War continued for seven years, and toward the end, the shortage of sailors became a serious problem for the English. In fact, it was not uncommon for them to be so short-handed that some ships couldn't sail. On one occasion, press gangs snatched four hundred men in British-held New York City so English vessels could leave the harbor.

The English navy was an important factor in Britain's plans to put down the rebellion in the colonies. Almost everything British soldiers wore, ate, or used in battle had to be supplied by British ships. And even when American privateers increased their number of raids, the British could not stop their shipments to the colonies. To do that was to end their army's ability to fight, even to survive.

And so British and American sailors tried to outwit, outrun, or overtake each other throughout the war. In doing so, many repeatedly risked their lives.

EDITOR'S NOTE

American sailors, like Andrew Sherburne, encountered adventure, danger, and incredible hardships as they struggled with the British navy, and these events created lasting impressions. Years after the war, when he was over sixty, Andrew wrote an autobiography titled *The Memoirs of Andrew Sherburne, A Pensioner of the Navy of the Revolution*. His book, published in 1828, contains stories about the war, his lifelong search for God and a religious faith in which he could believe, as well as the major events of his adult life.

The present book contains only part of Andrew's original memoirs, his adventures during the war. In Sherburne's preface, he stated that one of his purposes for writing his book was to help his countrymen appreciate their freedom more by understanding what it cost the soldiers and sailors to win that freedom. The events selected for this book — and told in Andrew's own words — were chosen to give young readers today a sense of what it was like to be alive and involved in history as it was being created well over 200 years ago. I eliminated most of his text regarding religion because it did not deal directly with events in the war and consisted mostly of rambling essays that were difficult to understand. The events of his adult life are summarized very briefly in the afterword here.

The colonists did not write or speak exactly as we do, and Andrew used terms such as "to discover a want of fortitude" (to recognize a lack of courage) or "put off the effeminate mourner" (to stop his unmanly crying), which are not familiar to us today. In most cases, his words are made clear by the context in which they are used. However, some are not easily understood by text alone. These words have been defined or located in the glossary, and they appear in italics the first time they are used in the text. In a few cases, I substituted modern words for Andrew's colonial terms to avoid confusion and misunderstanding.

Also, Andrew made a number of references to places as he traveled from one site to another. In most cases, he gave the modern name as well as the old, if the name changed over time. However, he mentioned a city called Lime as he headed north from Boston in the third episode. There is no modern-day city named Lime in the area, and it's most likely that he meant Lynn.

And finally, as in all autobiographies, the author has described the events as he remembered them, and he has described himself as he would like to be remembered. Another person at the same events—a British sailor or a merchant attacked by privateers, for example—would tell a different tale. Nevertheless, few could deny that Andrew saw lots of action in the war and repeatedly showed courage when facing the enemy.

K. Z.

Revolutionary War in the Colonies

These are the major events of the war taking place either before Andrew Sherburne begins his adventures or during his hazardous tour. They provide a framework in which to read the text that follows.

1775   ☆ The first battles of the war take place at Lexington and Concord, Massachusetts.

☆ Boston, Massachusetts, is taken by British forces.

☆ The Continental Congress makes plans to start a navy.

1776   ☆ Charleston, South Carolina, is attacked by the British under Sir Peter Parker. Parker fails to capture the city.

☆ The English take New York City and the surrounding area.

☆ General Washington captures Trenton, New Jersey.

1777 ☆ The British take Philadelphia, Pennsylvania, the patriots' capital, but they lose heavily at Saratoga, New York.

☆ Washington and his men spend the winter at Valley Forge.

1778 ☆ The British again turn their attention to the southern colonies where they believe they have strong support from Loyalists or Tories, men and women in the colonies who support the king. The English take Savannah and Augusta, Georgia.

1779 ☆ The Americans try to recapture Savannah for almost a year. They fail.

1780 ☆ Charleston, South Carolina is taken by the British.

1781 ☆ British forces under Lord Cornwallis lose at Yorktown, Virginia. About 7,000 British soldiers surrender, and the fighting ends in the colonies.

1782 ☆ A peace treaty is signed by both sides.

1783 ☆ The treaty is ratified by Congress in April. The British free the rest of their prisoners in New York and Charleston and leave both cities.

MEMOIRS

OF

ANDREW SHERBURNE

A PENSIONER OF THE

NAVY OF THE REVOLUTION

———

WRITTEN BY HIMSELF

———

"They that go down to the sea in ships, that do business in great waters:
they see the works of the LORD, and his wonders in the deep."
Psalmist.

PREFACE

The author of this little narrative is among the few surviving actors in a revolution which gave freedom and prosperity to the great republic of North America. He sees his contemporaries rapidly falling around him and bending beneath the weight of years and early sufferings. He feels that the hour when he shall go the way of all the earth cannot be far distant.

Under such circumstances, he is impressed with the idea that he still owes a duty to his country and his children. In this narrative, he has endeavored to unite the discharge of these duties. He has given his countrymen a plain, unvarnished tale of the sufferings of those who, in the war of our independence, sustained the cause of liberty in the tented field or on the mountain wave. Most fervently does he wish that Americans may properly appreciate the freedom which they enjoy while they learn the price of its purchase.

With reference to his children, he is not ashamed to confess that the avails which may arise from the sale of this humble performance must be almost their only inheritance. Those early years which others employ in acquiring wealth or knowledge, in the case of the author, passed away amidst the hardships of a sailor's life or were lingered out in prison.

With much diffidence, he submits this work to the public. Candid men will not expect elegance of style from one who has been denied the advantages of an education.

ANDREW SHERBURNE
AUGUSTA, NEW YORK
JULY 15, 1828

ONE

Eager to Try
My Fortune at Sea

I was born in the town of Rye, once a part of Portsmouth, New Hampshire, September 30, 1765. Rye is within one hundred *rods* of the Atlantic Ocean.

The celebrated *Stamp Act* passed the British Parliament in 1765, the year of my birth. This act excited a general alarm among the American colonists, and resolutions were passed against it by most of the colonial assemblies.

I had breathed but a few days when ten of the colonies, by their representatives, formed a *Colonial Congress*. This took place in the city of New York in October, 1765.

And I was about nine years of age and living in Londonderry, New Hampshire, when the British took possession of Boston, which has been termed "The Cradle of American Independence." The seizure of Boston exacerbated the feelings of the colonists in every section of our country.

The conflict at Bunker Hill and the burning of Charlestown, Massachusetts, further roused the Irish Yankees of

Londonderry. The young men went off to the battleground, prompted by their sires who followed them with their horses laden with provisions, and I wished myself old enough to take an active part in this contest. Little did I realize at that time the horrors of war. I had not yet heard the clash of arms, the groans of the dying, and the shouts of the victors.

A martial spirit was diffused throughout the little circle of my acquaintances. The men were frequently called together for the purpose of acquiring military discipline, and their example was not lost upon the boys. Lads from seven years old and upwards were formed into companies, and being properly officered, armed with wooden guns, and adorned with plumes, they would go through the manual exercise with as much regularity as the men.

When I returned to Portsmouth in 1778, many new objects were presented to my view. Ships were being built, prizes taken from the enemy unloaded, and privateers fitted out. Nearby, soldiers drilled, and the roar of cannon and the sound of martial music so infatuated me, I was once again filled with anxiety to become an actor in the scenes of war.

My eldest brother, Thomas, had just returned from a cruise on board the *General Mifflin* of Boston. This ship had captured thirteen prizes, some of which, being of little value, were burned. A few were sold in France, and the others were taken to Boston where their cargoes were divided among the crew.

After hearing about my brother's adventures, I became even more eager to try my fortune at sea. Though not yet

fourteen years of age, like other boys, I imagined myself almost a man. I had intimated to my sister that if my father would not consent that I should go to sea, I would run away and go on board a privateer. My mind became so obsessed with the subject that I talked of it in my sleep and was overheard by my mother. She communicated what she had heard to my father.

My parents were apprehensive that I might wander off and go on board some vessel without their consent. At that time, it was not an uncommon thing for lads to come out of the country, step on board a privateer, make a cruise, and return home, their friends remaining in ignorance of their fate until they heard it from the boys themselves. Others would pack up their clothes, take a hunk of cheese and a loaf of bread, and steer off for the army.

A Continental ship of war, the *Ranger* of eighteen guns, commanded by Thomas Simpson, was shipping a crew in Portsmouth at this time. The *Ranger* had been ordered to join two *frigates*, the *Boston* and the *Providence*, and the *Queen of France*, a ship of twenty guns, upon an expedition directed by Congress.

My father, having consented that I should go to sea, preferred the service of Congress to privateering. He was acquainted with Captain Simpson, and my two half-uncles, Timothy and James Weymouth, were on the *Ranger*. As most of its principal officers belonged to the town, Portsmouth parents preferred this station for their sons who were about to enter the naval service, and there were probably thirty local boys on board.

My father and I visited the *Ranger*, and placing much dependence on the protection of my uncles, I shipped as one of her crew. I was elated with my supposed good fortune which had at last made me a sailor.

The boys were employed in waiting on the officers, but in time of action, each boy was to carry cartridges to a particular gun. I was waiter to Charles Roberts, the *boatswain*, and I was quartered at the third gun from the bow.

Being ready for sea, we sailed to Boston and joined the *Providence*, the *Boston*, and the *Queen of France*. I believe that this small *squadron* composed nearly the entire navy of the United States.

We proceeded to sea sometime in June, 1779. A considerable part of the crew of the *Ranger* had no sailing experience, and the sea was rough, especially in the *Gulf Stream*. Many were exceedingly sick, myself among the rest, and we afforded a subject of constant ridicule to the old sailors. We cruised several weeks, made the *Western Islands*, and at length fell in with the homeward-bound Jamaica fleet off the *banks* of Newfoundland.

It was our practice to keep a man at the *masthead* constantly on the lookout. The moment a sail was discovered, a signal was given to our *consorts*, and all possible exertion was made to come up to the stranger or discover what she was. About seven o'clock one morning, the man at the masthead cried out, "A sail! A sail on the lee bow! Another there and there!"

Our young officers ran up the *shrouds*, and with their glasses, they soon ascertained that more than fifty sail could be seen. The Jamaica fleet, which consisted of about 150 sail, some of which were armed, was *convoyed* by one or two *lines* of battleships, several frigates and *sloops of war*. Our little squadron was in the rear of the fleet. Suddenly my mind was agitated with alternate hopes and fears.

We pursued a large ship, and in the course of an hour, we came up with the *Holderness*, a three-decker mounting twenty-two guns. She *struck* after we gave her several *broadsides*. Although she had more guns than we did, her crew was not sufficiently large to manage them and, at the same time, work the ship. She was loaded with cotton, coffee, sugar, rum, and allspice.

It was now nearly night, but we were unwilling to abandon the opportunity of enriching ourselves. We kept going under easy sail.

During the summer months, it is often extremely foggy on the banks of Newfoundland, and a ship cannot be seen at the distance of one hundred yards. Then in a few moments, you may have a clear sky and bright sun for half an hour. When the sun finally shone the next day, it enabled us to see a numerous fleet a few miles away. But it was in such a compact order that we thought it best not to approach it. We were, however, hoping that we might pick up some single ship. We eventually spotted a lone ship just before dark, and we took and manned out a *brig*.

Although I had been at sea for some time now, I still wasn't used to the maxims or dialect of sailors, and my earlier aversion to swearing had rendered me an object of ridicule. I had been insulted and frequently obliged to fight. My uncles had prompted me to defend my rights, and as my boxing improved, I was sometimes victorious. Nevertheless, I finally decided to indulge in swearing. I eventually persuaded myself that there was a necessity for it, and now I had became proficient in this abominable practice. My swearing caused some remorse, and to counterbalance my guilt, I became more constant in praying. Before, I had only prayed occasionally. Now I prayed every night to atone for the sins of the day, and this night was no exception.

The next day, we gained sight of three ships to which we gave chase. When they discovered us in pursuit, they huddled together, intending, we supposed, to fight. However, they soon made sail and ran from us. After a short lapse of time, we overhauled and took one of them, which we soon found to be a dull sailer. Another, while we were manning our prize, attempted to escape, but we gained upon her.

While in chase, two large ships hove in sight. One of them shaped her course for us, the other for the prize we had just manned. We were unwilling to give up our chase and return to the prize as we had learned that the other ships, unarmed, were laden with sugar, rum, and cotton. We soon came up with the hindmost, brought her to, and ordered her to keep under our stern while we might pursue the other.

The ship in chase of us was under English *colors*, but we soon ascertained by her signal that she was our *Providence* on board of which was our commodore. This joyful intelligence relieved us from all fear, and we soon came up with our chase.

In the meantime, the prize under our stern sought to get under the protection of the *Providence*, mistaking that frigate for one of the English convoy. Our prize eluded us, hailed our commodore, and informed him that a Yankee cruiser had taken one of the fleet.

"Very well, very well," replied the commodore. "I'll be along side of her directly." He then hauled down his English colors, hoisted the American, and ordered the ship to come under his stern. This order was obeyed immediately.

We now discovered the identity of the strange ship which was in chase of our first prize. It was another of our consorts, the *Queen of France*.

Having manned our prizes and secured our prisoners, we shaped our course for Boston. We arrived sometime in the last of July or the beginning of August, 1779.

The *Ranger* made but a short stop at Boston, for as most of our officers and crew belonged to Portsmouth and its vicinity, our vessel could be most conveniently refitted there. The cargoes from our ten prizes were divided among our crews. My share was about one ton of sugar, from thirty to forty gallons of fourth-proof Jamaica rum, about twenty pounds of cotton, approximately twenty pounds of ginger, *logwood*, and allspice, and about $700 in paper money equal to one hundred dollars in *specie*.

On returning home, I had the satisfaction of finding my family well. Another sister had been added to the family, and my eldest brother had returned from a successful voyage in a merchantman. My readers must be left to imagine the feelings of my parents when they could number four sons and seven daughters around their table in health and prosperity.

TWO

An Attack on Charleston

After a few weeks, the *Ranger* was again ready for sea. The same officers and most of the same crew were going in her. We rejoined our consorts and cruised southward. After several months of searching, we had only taken a few small British transports of little value, and that winter, we took them to Charleston, South Carolina.

After replenishing our provisions and water, we put to sea on another cruise off the coast of Florida and the Southern colonies. About the middle of February, 1780, early in the morning, we discovered four or five large British ships of war to *leeward* of us, the land being in sight to *windward*. The enemy gave us chase. We beat up to Charleston Bar, came to anchor, and waited a little while for the tide to rise. Then we ran in and came to anchor under Ft. Moultrie at Sullivan's Island.

The British lay several days outside. Then they lightened their ships, came in over the bar, and came to anchor. But

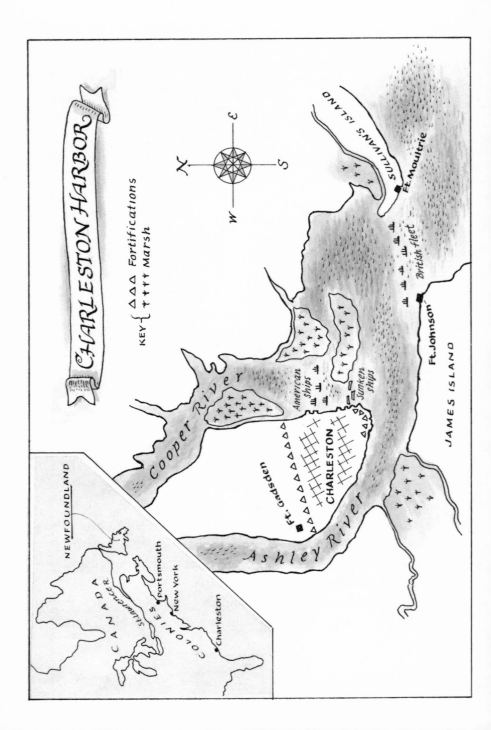

they durst not approach the fort. They doubtless recollected the defeat of Sir Peter Parker before the same fort in 1776.

It was now learned that the enemy planned an attack on Charleston. The harbor was completely blockaded, and the ships at the bar were soon joined by others.

The *Ranger*, being the smallest ship of our squadron, could approach near the shore, and it was ordered to attack a small *battery* that the enemy had erected upon James Island. Our ship came to anchor before the battery and commenced cannonading with great fury, and we continued the firing for an hour and a half without cessation. We succeeded in dismounting their cannon and obliging their soldiers to quit their ground. Our ship received several shots, but no person was injured.

At the commencement of the cannonading, I was exceedingly alarmed but was careful to conceal my fears from my shipmates. After we had discharged a few broadsides, my fears pretty much subsided, and I, with high spirits, carried cartridges to my gun until the firing ceased.

Later our little ship was detached to encounter a battery above the city. We commenced our firing a little before high water and were not as successful as we had been with the one on James Island. Our ship received a twenty-four-pound ball which lodged in her side directly against where I stood. It struck the salt marsh, which deadened its force, or it must have gone through the ship and would have killed me. We were forced to withdraw from our station shortly after the tide began to ebb, and we had to use our boats and small anchors to *warp* our ship into deeper water, there being little wind at that time.

Charleston was not so fortified as to stand a regular siege, and yet we were enabled to make a vigorous defense for a while. A chain of *redoubts*, lines and batteries, extended from the Ashley River to the Cooper River.

The British eventually crossed the Ashley, and they broke ground on the night of the first of April. They were within 800 yards of our lines.

About the ninth, the British fleet lying within the bar, having a fresh wind in its favor, ventured to run by Sullivan's Island under a heavy fire from Ft. Moultrie. The fleet lost twenty-seven seamen and one transport. The British anchored between the fort and the city, secure from the cannon of both.

Our ships could now no longer be employed to advantage, and their crews and some of their guns were removed into batteries. Captain Simpson and the *Ranger*'s crew were stationed in Fort Gadsden. This being the uppermost fort on the river, it was much exposed to the fire of the British. A bomb, at one time, fell within a few feet of me. Though much alarmed, I threw myself behind the carriage of a large gun and escaped unhurt.

The siege being closely pressed, balls and shells were continually falling within the city. During the night, I have counted ten bombs of different sizes flying in the air at one time. No spot could now be considered as a place of safety. We were in continual apprehension of an attempt to carry our works by storm, since the force of the enemy was far superior to ours.

Our provisions being exhausted, we capitulated on the twelfth day of May, 1780. Our officers were *paroled* and allowed to retain their waiters, and we were given permission to be at large within the city. We were entirely destitute of provisions for several days except for mussels, which we gathered from their beds.

The day after our surrender a distressing accident occurred. While some British soldiers were depositing muskets taken from us in a storeroom, the powder stored there exploded. The shock was tremendous and fatal to many who were instantly hurried into eternity. I saw the print of a man who had been dashed against the end of a brick church thirty feet from the ground, and perhaps thirty rods from the storeroom.

Shortly after, it was discovered that smallpox prevailed among the British troops. Few of the New Englanders had ever had that disease, and our officers deemed it advisable that we should be inoculated.

Our physicians performed this service for us. I much more dreaded this disease than I did the bombs of the enemy. When the symptoms came on, I was greatly alarmed, but I had them very favorably, and one of our officers, Captain Powers, did all he could for my relief.

THREE

I Feared I Should
Never Get Home

As soon as it was practical, Captain Simpson and other officers procured a small vessel to transport the officers, their boys, and their baggage from Charleston to Newport, Rhode Island. The British had agreed to this in the terms of capitulation.

Our passage to Rhode Island was rather long. It being difficult to procure suitable casks for water, the men obtained such as they could. The casks proved to be foul, and after we got to sea, our water became filthy and noxious. Very few on board escaped illness.

A considerable number of us having been exposed to smallpox, it was necessary that we should be thoroughly cleansed before passing through the countryside. There were little smokehouses erected on a remote part of Rhode Island for this purpose. Watched by police officers, we entered one, unpacked our clothes and scattered them all

about. We almost suffocated from a smoke made of oakum and tobacco before we were allowed to leave.

We then went to a creek to wash. As I could swim tolerably well, I ventured into the current. Some lads expressed their surprise at their inability to swim. Indeed, none of us were aware of our weakness. My feet got entangled in eelgrass and were drawn under water. Only by making every possible effort could I disengage them and recover the shore. No one could afford me any assistance.

Captain Powers hired a passage for himself and me to Boston in a two-horse wagon. The roads at that time were very different from what they are now, and the contrast between the motion of a vessel on water to that of a wagon over a rough road is very great. The jolting proved very unfavorable to us in our weak state, and when we arrived at our destination, the Cox house, Captain Powers was immediately confined to bed and placed under the care of a physician. Though weak and without appetite, I was able to keep about.

A friend of my grandmother's, an inhabitant of Boston, heard that part of the *Ranger*'s crew had arrived in the city. He called at the house while I was at the *apothecary*'s shop. He told Captain Powers that my father was dead. My captain was so deeply afflicted by this news, he asked Mrs. Cox to inform me rather than communicate the distressing news himself.

On my return, Mrs. Cox took me into another room, and with much sympathy, she made known to me the matter. I passed some time in tears and reflection.

I then went into my captain's chamber. He readily perceived that I had received the heart-rending news, and he was quite affected. Said he, "Andrew, you have met with a great loss. I am very sorry for you. I don't know how it will turn with me, but I hope you won't leave me. I suppose you are desirous to get home, but I am unwilling to part with you. I have no child, and if I should live and you will live with me, I will make you my son. I will do all I can for you."

This friendly address much affected me. I loved the man, and although I had a great desire to get home, I could not leave him. His time, however, was short. I think he died the next day, and I grieved for the loss of such a kind and faithful friend.

Mr. and Mrs. Cox felt much for me, and they tried to comfort me. They thought I had better try to get home. Mr. Cox said there was no *coaster* in from Portsmouth at that time and that there might not be any in for a week or more. He thought that if I set out by land, I would get some assistance in my journey of about sixty miles. Mr. Cox gave me five or six dollars and his best counsel and wishes, and tears flowed from Mrs. Cox's eyes while she gave me her benediction.

I set out in the fore part of the day, and with my little bag, I stalked down to the ferry. The ferryman had just arrived from the opposite shore, and my meager appearance immediately excited his attention. He went directly over with me without waiting for any other riders, and he gave me my passage.

My complaint had now become a confirmed dysentery, and I found myself poorly able to travel. I had not walked a mile before I was obliged to lie under a shade tree by the roadside. A train of melancholy reflections overwhelmed my mind. My father was dead, and my master was no more. I knew not whether I could rise on my feet, or if I could rise, whether I could walk. And I feared I should never get home. I wept bitterly until my tears were exhausted.

Finally I attempted to rise and, with difficulty, succeeded. I picked up my bag and slowly pursued my journey. I had walked too fast from the ferry and too far without resting. Now I walked cautiously and rested frequently.

As I was passing a house in Lime, I was noticed by a

woman who stood in her door. She came to the road, asked me a few questions, and insisted upon my going into the house. We were met at the door by another tender-hearted mother. One or both of them had a son in the army.

The best which their house afforded was at my service. I took sparingly of their refreshments and, in their presence, put off the effeminate mourner.

My spirits were revived now, and after I left the women I continued to walk slowly and rest frequently. I made good progress, and in about seven days, I arrived at Portsmouth.

Little did I expect to find such changes in my family in one year. My mother had only two of her children with her. One of my sisters was living with our uncle on the farm that had once belonged to my grandparents, and my brother Thomas had sailed for the West Indies in December with Captain Shores. The men had been gone long enough to have made two voyages to the islands, but there was no intelligence from them, nor has there ever been any to this day. Without doubt, they foundered in a violent gale which arose shortly after their departure.

My mother was employed in spinning, knitting, and sewing for others, her only means of supporting herself and the children who were with her. She would sit at her wheel for hours without uttering a word, while now and then the tears would roll down her cheeks. When she broke silence, she narrated some event which transpired in my father's day, or she referred to some event respecting her dear Thomas, her first born.

Nearly two months elapsed before I recovered so as to be capable of any business. My father left no estate, and the avails of my former cruise were pretty much exhausted. I was very desirous of doing something for my family, but there was no employment for me on shore unless I should go into the army. I preferred the sea.

FOUR

Privateering Had Become
the Order of the Day

After the *Ranger*, built in Portsmouth, had fallen into the hands of the enemy, local patriotic merchants built a beautiful ship to take her place. They called her the *Alexander* and gave Captain Simpson command of her. A considerable number of the *Ranger*'s officers and crew were to occupy the same stations they had held on board the *Ranger* on the new ship. I was invited by Captain Simpson to try my fortune with him again, and I readily accepted the offer.

We sailed from Portsmouth in December, 1780. Although we cruised upwards of three months, we took nothing. We never gave chase to any vessel without coming up with her, but we never met with an enemy. Our cruise was designed for three months, but as we could get no prize, we prolonged it. Our provision failed, and we came to half *allowance* before we got in. We really suffered for water.

The *Alexander* was preparing for her second cruise, and I had been invited to sail in her again when a circumstance occurred which gave me a different direction. I was walking the street one day, and being in seaman's garb, I was readily recognized as a sailor. Suddenly a jolly tar approached me.

"Ha, shipmate! Don't you wish to take a short cruise in a fine *schooner* and make your fortune?"

I replied that I expected to sail in the *Alexander.*

"Oh, we shall get back," said he, "before the *Alexander* will get ready to sail."

The young man was Captain Jacob Willis of Kennebunkport, Maine, and his privateer was called the *Greyhound.* She had been a bank fisherman, but now being finely painted and having a new and longer set of masts and spars and mounting four-pounders, she made quite a warlike appearance.

Privateering had now become the order of the day. In many instances, small vessels had as good success as large ones, though it was difficult to get a sufficient number of hands to man them.

Captain Willis told me he was going into York, a small port three *leagues* east of Portsmouth. If I would go with him and did not like the boat and crew, he promised to pay my expenses back to Portsmouth. Since I was almost sixteen and pretty well grown, he also promised that I should have a fair share of anything we took. These promises induced me to go on board as far as York.

Once on board, I found a jovial company. The *Greyhound* had a full complement of officers, two or three ordinary seamen, and between twenty and thirty boys, scarcely one of them as large as myself and some of them not a dozen years old. I was taken into the cabin by Captain Willis and his officers where I spent an enjoyable evening. In this, no doubt, there was a plan between Captain Willis and his men. I was not yet secured, and they wished that I might become attached to them.

The next day we ran down to York. Here it became necessary for Captain Willis to lay some plan to increase his crew, for in Portsmouth he had had very poor success. Willis decided to get up a frolic at a public house. People were hired to invite lads and lasses for a country dance, and rum, coffee, sugar, and biscuits were taken on shore from the privateer for the party.

The frolic was large, and it became necessary to have dancing in more than one room. Having but one fiddler, I was selected to sing for some of the dancers. This suited my turn, for I was not proficient in dancing.

Every art and insinuation was employed by the officers to obtain recruits. Still, they succeeded in getting only two that evening.

The next day was one of the most memorable days of my life. Gloom and horror fell upon my mind, and it is impossible for me to describe what I felt or to explain why I felt so despondent. Suddenly the voyage before me looked as gloomy as death. I resolved to return home, but even in this resolution I could not anticipate the least degree of relief. I disclosed my intention to Captain Willis. He engaged his officers to persuade me to stay and spend one more evening with them. They were so urgent, I reluctantly gave my consent.

The captain was satisfied that this was not the place for him to make up his crew, and he was determined to push

farther eastward. I gave my consent to go on the cruise. We left York and sailed to Kennebunkport. Here we obtained one hand. His name was Samuel Willis, a kinsman of the captain, a lad about sixteen years old.

We then sailed to Falmouth, which is now called Portland. We made but a short stop in the port and got only one hand, and a poor thing he was. There was now no further prospect of increasing our crew, and we were obliged to try our luck with what we had.

I very much regretted that I had ever seen the *Greyhound*. My melancholy, which commenced at York, had by no means subsided, and at times, I felt fearful forebodings. But I endeavored to put the best side out, for it was by no means becoming a young sailor to discover a want of fortitude.

We ventured to take a peep into Halifax, Nova Scotia. As we drew near the harbor, we discovered a ship, apparently in distress, aiming to get in. We hoped she might be a prize for us. We were not, however, without suspicion, and the nearer we approached her the more our suspicion increased. At length, we thought it best to draw off. We had no sooner shifted our course than she got up her topgallant yard, set her sails, and gave us chase. She gained on us, and we began to dread Halifax prison. She chased us for several hours, but fortunately for us, it became foggy, and by maneuvering, we eluded her.

Our captain now thought it best to try our luck on the Eastern shore and about the mouth of the St. Lawrence River. As we proceeded, we could look in no direction without seeing a sail, and we were at a loss to determine whether they were friends or foes. However, having spoken with one or two captains, we learned that they were all Americans.

The next day, we visited the island of St. Pierre at the mouth of Fortune Bay in Newfoundland. Near this island, we fell in with a Newfoundland *shallop*. We examined the owner very closely, and we were informed by him that an English brig, with supplies for the fishing stations, had recently entered the bay.

We flattered ourselves that we should fall in with this brig and obtain a fine prize. We sailed up the bay, visiting several ports where fishing was carried on upon a large scale, but we found nothing of the brig.

Having failed in our enterprise, our captain took two of the best shallops he could find, which belonged to merchants in England. He loaded them with oil and dry fish, property of the same merchants.

These shallops were committed to the care of Captain Arnold. He went on board the largest of them with two hands, James Annis and me. Jasper Loyd, an old Cape Ann fisherman, had charge of the other shallop (subject to Captain Arnold), and with him were Samuel Willis and Samuel Babb. We left the *Greyhound* in Fortune Bay and set out for Salem, Massachusetts.

FIVE

A Critical Situation

After we set out for Salem, the wind headed us, and we were forced to put back and anchor in the bay. We lay wind bound several days.

One morning when I came on deck, I perceived that Captain Arnold was very different. He had appeared low spirited from the time we left the *Greyhound*, and now he appeared, in some measure, deranged.

In the evening, he asked me to get a light and come into his cabin. I complied with his request and tarried with him all night. Neither of us slept any, and he talked without cessation upon almost every subject imaginable. Sometimes he would seem to talk rationally, and then he would appear completely deranged again. I had the impression that he had an awful dread of falling into the hands of the enemy.

In the morning, he appeared very cheerful and full of business. But in the course of the day, he seemed to imagine himself on board the privateer, and he would frequently speak to other officers and reply as though they answered him.

When night came on, I advised him to go into his cabin. I made his bed and told him to lie down. He complied without hesitation after giving me some papers to safeguard, and then he was still. I was determined to secure him, so I shut the door and buttoned it on the outside. I then took a long stick of wood, seven or eight inches in diameter, set one end against the door and the other high against a bulkhead and pressed the stick down with my whole weight. I thought the door perfectly secure, and having had no sleep the night before, I turned in.

In the morning, the other hand, James Annis, went on deck but soon returned in great surprise. He woke me saying, "Sherburne, where is Captain Arnold?"

I said that he was in his cabin.

"He is not on board," said Annis.

I immediately went on deck and saw the open cabin door. I looked in and could find nothing of the captain. All his clothes lay on deck except his waistcoat. My readers can imagine my surprise and distress on this awful occasion!

The other shallop was within fifty yards of us, and Loyd and his hands had a *skiff*. We hailed them and informed them of the circumstances and asked them to come with the little boat, which they did. We went round and round the shallop, enlarging our circle and viewing the bottom very carefully. We saw nothing unusual.

Then we went on shore and walked on the beach to see if we could discover any tracks of bare feet in the sand. All our endeavors to find Captain Arnold failed.

The question now was, what shall we do? Loyd was no navigator, though he was well acquainted with the Eastern shore. His plan was to take both shallops under his command and try to get them to Salem. He flattered himself that he should have a decent share if he should succeed. I proposed that we should all board the best shallop and take the sails and light rigging off the other and use them to make our way home. The old man would not consent.

I felt myself in a critical situation. Annis knew not a point of the compass, had never attempted to steer the ship, and knew nothing about working the vessel. The wind was yet against us. We were in an enemy's country, and we had to cross the gulf of the St. Lawrence River and get by Halifax. The thought of taking charge of this little vessel and taking her to Salem with Annis with all these difficulties together with the uncertainty of the weather was extremely upsetting. The inflexibility, folly, and unfriendliness of old Mr. Loyd increased my perplexity as well as my resentment. But he had the advantage of me, and I was obliged to submit.

I do not know that I slept any that night. My thoughts were much employed upon Captain Arnold, his wife, and his children. I retraced the trials through which I had passed, and I attempted to look forward, but all was darkness.

The next day, the wind was more favorable, and we got under weigh. Annis could assist me in getting up the anchor and hoisting the sails, but he knew not how to trim them to the wind.

Towards night, I spoke with Mr. Loyd and entreated him to consider my situation. I pleaded with him to let Samuel

Willis come on board with me and to take Annis on board with him. To this he agreed.

Early in the evening, we had something of a breeze, and it continued to increase throughout the night. By midnight we had quite a gale. The night was dark, and neither moon nor stars could be seen. We earnestly wished for day.

When day came, we discovered more visibly our danger.

The clouds looked wild and the ocean rough. We had lost the skiff, which was towing at our stern, and at sunrise, we split our mainsail from top to bottom. Our foremast was now in great danger from having so much sail upon it. The wind was not steady, but blew in gusts, and when a heavy one came, our foremast would bend like a whip. Our vessel was heavy laden, and she labored hard in so rough a sea.

This caused her to leak, keeping one of us bailing most of the time while the other stood at the helm.

We were very fearful that we could not weather the gale, and every moment we expected that our mast would go over the bow. In that case, we should have foundered in a few minutes.

Around noon, we discovered an island directly ahead of us. We ventured to bear off a little, but we could not possibly look clear of it. The time was short, for we were running at least at the rate of twelve or fourteen miles an hour. But as we drew near, our case looked more favorable. We cleared the island by perhaps twenty yards, and as soon as we passed it, we drew immediately up under its lee.

The other shallop arrived about the same time. We all finally came to anchor in a small cove.

Willis stayed with me that night, but he told me he should not go to sea again in our shallop. It was my determination to quit the shallop if Willis did. Although I had but one night's rest in four, I did not sleep much on this night, knowing what must take place on the morrow. I had nothing to fear from Willis, Babb, or Annis, but I expected to find Mr. Loyd in a hostile temper.

S I X

They Soon Began to Fire Upon Us

The next morning, Willis went on board his own vessel again, and I went with him. I asked Mr. Loyd what we should do.

"Do?" said he. "Why, I must help you mend your mainsail, and you must try it again."

I remonstrated against the measure. I said that Willis declined continuing with me and that it was out of the question to think of getting both shallops home. I finally told him plainly that I had quit my shallop and was determined to stay on board his vessel.

He began to swear, and he threatened me. I told him that I disregarded his threats and that I was willing to do my duty, but only on his ship. No one interfered, and the old gentleman finally began to be moderate. However, he was determined to take the other shallop in tow.

In short, we got under weigh, and in the course of an hour or two, we discovered a small schooner making towards us. We were all convinced she was an enemy except Mr. Loyd. We tried to persuade him to cut the shallop adrift and try to be off with one, but he declined.

The schooner's crew soon began to fire upon us. The first time they did so, they did not strike us, but we heard their bullets whistle over our heads. The second time they fired, their charge went through the top of our mainsail.

In a few minutes, they were along side of us, and twenty men sprang on board with long guns in their hands, loaded, cocked, and primed. They presented two or three at each of our breasts, cursing us bitterly, and threatening

us. We pleaded for quarter, but they seemed determined to take our lives.

One or two men, including their commander, interceded for us. However, such entreaties seemed to increase the rage of some of the men. We stood trembling, awaiting their decisions. At length, their captain, and several others who appeared more rational, prevailed.

Their first business was to get their prizes under weigh for their port which was called Grand Bank. The wind being fair, we arrived before night.

We were taken on shore and soon surrounded, perhaps by a hundred people. Amongst them was an old English lady who appeared to have an excellent education and to whose opinion and instruction they all seemed to pay a special deference. She was the only person amongst them who inquired after papers.

I presented the *letters* that Captain Arnold had given to me for safekeeping. This lady took the papers and commenced to read them out loud without interruption until she came to the clause which authorized us to "burn, sink, or destroy" enemy ships. Many of the people became so exasperated when they heard this, they swore we ought to be killed outright.

The old lady soon called them to order. She informed them that the papers made us prisoners of war and that we ought to be treated with humanity and conveyed to a British armed station.

This good woman gave directions, and a few of the villagers prepared some refreshment for us. They hung a pot over a fire and boiled some corned codfish and salted pork.

When the fish and meat were cooked sufficiently, the villagers took the pot outside where there was a square piece of board which had a cleat on each edge, the corners being open. They turned the pot upside down upon the board, and when the water had drained away, the board was set on a table. We stood round this table without plates or forks and picked up our food with our fingers.

Having taken our refreshment, we were conducted into a cooper's shop and locked up. We tried to compose ourselves as well as we could.

The next morning, we were put on board a shallop. Everything was taken from us except what we had upon our backs. Even our shoes were taken from our feet. We sailed up the bay as far as a small harbor called Cornish.

The following morning, we sailed six or eight miles up a river and landed in order to strike out for Placentia Bay. We were guarded by seven sturdy fellows with long muskets. Some of the fellows were very rude and not a little abusive. They said the distance overland to Placentia Bay was twenty miles.

We marched through a dreary wilderness. The timber was small, but there was an abundance of briars and craggy underbrush, which was very injurious to our legs and bare feet. Poor Mr. Loyd was most to be pitied, for he began to lag early in the day and frequently received heavy blows from the breeches of the guards' guns. In the course of the day, we each received a hard biscuit and a small slice of raw pork. It was night when we got over to the shore of the bay, and we were yet four or five miles from the station where there was a small battery and a few regular soldiers.

The little port we stopped at was occupied by a rich man who had a considerable number of shallops and fishermen employed in his service. Some of them had been treated rudely by American privateers, and the man was very upset when he learned that we were American prisoners. He insisted that we ought to be put to death immediately. He said that he would not supply us with anything to eat or give us shelter for the night.

But our guards had received their instructions from the old lady, and they threatened to present him to his majesty's officers if he wouldn't help. The old man abruptly quitted them and went to his house.

The guards then took possession of the old man's brew house in which he had been working that day. The floor was wet and muddy, so I went out and broke off fir and spruce boughs for my bed and lay down to rest. I was exceedingly tired and sore.

Some of the guards were busy getting something to eat. They procured plenty of corned codfish and boiled it. One of them came to me, gave me a shake, and bade me arise and eat my supper. Although I had had a scanty dinner, I was so tired, I declined to get up. The guard gave me a heavy thump and said, "Get up, Yankee, and take your supper."

I thought it best to comply with his commands. I arose and went to the table. It was sufficiently long for our whole company to stand round it. Although we had no plates, knives or forks, we did have several saucers of sweet oil on the table. Each man took some fish with his fingers, dipped it in oil, and ate it. I had great difficulty swallowing the fish, for the oil was offensive to my taste. I ate a few mouthfuls without oil and a small piece of ship bread and then very gladly returned to my bed of boughs.

In the morning, we walked four or five miles to the little battery. (I think it was called Morteer.) Our walk was much more distressing than it had been the day before. We were very stiff when we began our march, and our bare feet were sore. We had to pass over a promontory, and the ascent was difficult and tiresome, and the descent was dangerous. We had to catch and hold fast to bushes to avoid falling headlong upon the rocks below.

When we arrived in Morteer, the soldiers at the battery fired one of their pieces of artillery to show their joy. They were happy some Yankee prisoners had fallen into their hands. They also had been visited by American privateers, and the inhabitants' stores and shallops had been plundered.

From Morteer, we were taken to Burin and put on a boat bound for Placentia. Our old guard of seven men returned to Grand Bank.

We arrived at Placentia some time before night. One of the guards on our boat went to shore in a skiff and gave information of us.

Shortly after, the government boat came and took us to shore to the *commissary*'s house. We were conducted into a room by ourselves, and in a few minutes, the commissary came in with several other gentlemen who examined us.

They appeared to be gentlemen of refined sensibility, and they deeply regretted the discord which existed between England and the colonies. Their feelings were much

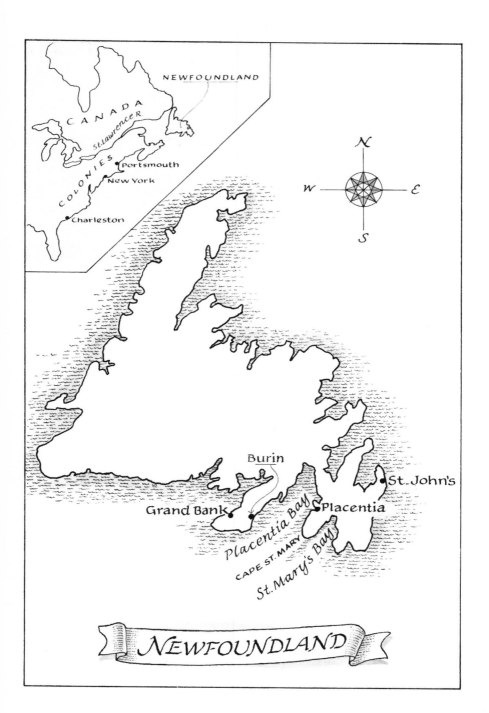

NEWFOUNDLAND

NEWFOUNDLAND

CANADA

St.Lawrence R.

COLONIES

Portsmouth

New York

Charleston

N

W E

S

Burin

St. John's

Grand Bank

Placentia Bay

Placentia

CAPE ST.MARY

St.Mary's Bay

NEWFOUNDLAND

hurt at seeing the condition of our feet, and they gave us some stockings and shoes. The commissary told us that we must stay in the garrison. He withdrew and sent us some bread and butter.

Soon after we had eaten, we heard the sound of bagpipes at the door, and we were taken into custody by a sergeant's guard of Highlanders in their kilts, plaids, Scotch bonnets and checkered stockings, accoutered with guns and fixed bayonets. I had seen the like before in Charleston, South Carolina, but to most of our company this was a novel sight. Babb, Annis, and Willis gazed with astonishment at the singular appearance of those soldiers.

We were conducted into the fort and confined to the guard room. It was perhaps sometime in May 1781, that we came to this place, and the season passed away until September without any prospect of release.

SEVEN

A Most Terrifying Scene

About the middle of September, a twenty-two-gun ship called the *Duchess of Cumberland* came to Placentia to convoy some English ships with cargoes of fish for Europe. While this ship lay in the harbor, one of her men deserted. Diligent search was made, but he could not be found. It was suspected that some of the inhabitants had concealed him, so the officers of the *Duchess* impressed one of the inhabitants by the name of Baggs in his stead.

We were put on board the *Duchess* to be taken to St. John's, Newfoundland, where there was a considerable number of prisoners. It was expected that there would be a *cartel* sent from St. John's to Boston for a prisoner exchange later that fall. Thus there appeared some prospect of our getting home again.

On our third day at sea, we had something of a blow and rain. When the wind increased more, it became necessary to close *reef* the topsails. At about three or four o'clock, the crew thought it had passed Cape St. Mary's, and Mr. Baggs, who had been skipper of a shallop for twenty years, was then invited to take his station on the forecastle, the station of the most accomplished seamen. Baggs asked the helmsman what course the ship was running, and when he ascertained it, he said, "If we run that course two hours, the ship will be on shore!"

At this, the sailors were alarmed, and they advised Baggs to give his information to the officers. He went to the quarter-deck and informed the officers that he was well acquainted with the coast, and that in his judgment, the ship and the men's lives were in danger.

But the British officers felt above being instructed by a Newfoundland fisherman. They commanded Baggs to be off the quarter-deck or they would kick him off. Mr. Baggs left, not a little chagrined.

At about five o'clock, there were loud and repeated cries from the forecastle. "Breakers on the lee bow! Breakers ahead!"

Immediately from the quarter-deck the following was heard, pronounced with emphasis. "Stand by to about ship! Hard to lee, fore sheet, fore top bowline, jib and staysail sheets, let go!" As the ship rounded to, head to the wind, it was pushed against a rugged bluff of rocks fifteen or twenty feet above the water. The *Duchess* struck with such violence, her *rudder* was broken off. The man at the helm was knocked overboard, and he was immediately dashed against the bluff. Two men near him managed to jump to safety on a rocky ledge.

I was going up the fore hatchway when the ship struck,

and looking down into the hold, I saw water gushing up in a stream eight or ten inches in diameter. With difficulty, I gained the quarter-deck where a most terrifying scene was presented to my view. The ship rolled so much her yard-arms nearly touched the water. The sea was breaking feather white all around us, and the rain descended in torrents. Some of the officers were raving and swearing. Others were crying and praying.

Orders were given to cut away the masts. Upon their fall, the ship cleared from the rock and drifted towards the shore, thumping against rocks, which lay under water, with tremendous force, throwing us about and against each other at a most dreadful rate.

In our course, we were brought up by some rocks which were so near the surface of the water, the ship could not get over them. She lay parallel with the shore, and every wave that came gave her a tremendous shock, and her decks began to open.

It became necessary to contrive some method of escape. There was no possibility of swimming to shore, and it was equally impossible for anyone to save himself on boards or broken pieces of the ship.

By this time, the two sailors who jumped on the rocks had somehow worked their way to shore. A small spar was procured, and a large rope was tied to it and hove over the stern. The waves carried the spar on shore, about eight rods away, and the men eventually succeeded in getting it. They tied the rope fast around a rock as large as a small haystack. Then the sailors on board drew the rope as tight as possible and made it fast around the stump of the foremast. There now seemed some small degree of hope. We could pull ourselves to safety along the rope, though when the waves ran, they would bury it ten feet or more under water.

The first man then attempted to go on shore. He appeared to do very well until he got about two rods from the ship where he was washed off the rope.

The next man who tried went the same way, and the fate of the two men discouraged any further attempt for sometime. At length, however, a third man tried, and he succeeded in getting on shore, where he was joyfully received.

I believe that ten reached the shore by the rope and four had been washed off, when I began to think of trying it myself. I took hold of the rope and fell into the water. The first wave, which was obstructed by the ship, buried me for a short time.

When the second wave came, I was exposed to its whole violence. I was stretched out straight horizontally, as if I had been suspended in air. Before the current abated, my right hand gave way. I then felt my left hand and arm faltering, and I expected to be immediately in eternity. But the undertow swept me beneath the rope. I then hove my right arm over it, gripped fast the collar of my jacket, and made all possible exertion to draw myself toward the shore.

The third wave stretched me, but having my arm over the rope, I was better fortified. Now I could almost touch the rocks below with my feet.

The fourth wave floated me, but its strength was almost spent before it reached me. As soon as it withdrew, two sailors followed it out, each holding the rope with one hand, and they drew me upon the beach. I had not strength for a time to move hand or foot.

By the time I was able to walk, the men had found a better method to get the sailors on shore. The middle of a long rope, one end on the ship, the other on shore, was made fast round a man's body. When the man fell into the water, the men on land would run with their end, and those on board would pay out their length, taking care to keep it taut to prevent the man from dashing against the rocks. Once the sailor was on the beach, he was untied, and part of the rope was pulled back to the ship and another man secured. More than one hundred men were drawn to safety this way.

But darkness came on before all could be pulled ashore. There were probably thirty yet on the wreck, including Mr. Loyd and Annis.

Our next object was to render our situation as comfortable as possible. We ascended the mountain near the beach about ten or fifteen yards and came to a kind of hollow. There was not sufficient room here for all to lie down without lying one upon another, but this we found to be most in our favor. Although it was quite uncomfortable for one man to have one or two others lying on him for a while, it was better than to be all the while exposed to the storm. Sometimes there were two lying on me. At other times, there was one under me and another on me, and sometimes I had two under me. We were obliged to interchange our stations frequently, for when underneath, we were too hard pressed, and when outside, the rain and cold were very severe. About two o'clock in the morning, the rain abated.

As daylight appeared, we rejoiced when we learned that the ship had not gone to pieces. We could converse with those on the wreck, and we planned to get on board when the tide, which was falling fast, should be down.

At about eight or nine o'clock, some men got on the wreck, and soon after, I went on myself. The hold was entirely empty. Every cask, all her *ballast*, and every other article had washed out. But in one of the *staterooms*, we found about two hundred pounds of bread, unhurt, and under the forecastle, we located two hundred pounds of meat. We also found a number of blankets in the sailors' hammocks, and the arm chest on the quarter-deck still contained muskets, some ammunition, tomahawks, and cutlasses, all of which were taken to shore.

It now became our object to ascertain how to get away. Mr. Baggs, whose counsel had been despised an hour before the ship struck, was now held in high estimation and looked up to even by the captain.

We were on the eastern side of Cape St. Mary's, perhaps ten miles from the head of the cape. Our station was against the side of a steep mountain whose height was five or six hundred feet. The shore was very bold, and it was what sailors generally call "ironbound." In some places the rocks were almost perpendicular, ten, twenty, and sometimes, forty feet high.

After we had eaten some bread and raw meat, a company of five or six men was selected to try to find its way up the mountain. In a zigzag direction, the men reached the summit and then came down as far as they could with safety. They stuck a crowbar into the ground and made fast a rope to it, and then they descended by the rope, making one rope fast to another until they got down.

It was one or two o'clock when we all began to ascend the mountain. When I reached the summit, I found myself on the border of a spacious plain. Not a tree or shrub could be seen to the north or west, but in the south there was a wilderness of evergreens. The ground was covered with a long, thick moss in which my feet would sink six inches at every step.

We took up our march for the woods, our company being something like 150 men, and it was about sunset when we got there. We tried to make some fire, but we had poor luck. The rain had wet everything. Although we stowed pretty close together and covered ourselves with blankets, we were very uncomfortable, for our clothes had scarcely got dry, and it was a frosty night.

In the morning, the captain and other officers had a long consultation with Mr. Baggs respecting the route we should pursue. It was concluded to shape our course to Placentia, which was something like a hundred miles away. We remained where we were that day in order that Mr. Baggs might examine the coast to settle some question in his mind.

Before we began our march the next day, the officers collected all provisions. All men were to receive an equal allowance. Three times a day the captain would deal out a small quantity of bread to each man, and another officer would distribute a small piece of meat.

We arrived at a little port, Point Var, on the eighth or ninth day. A few of our company were so exhausted they were left by the way. Whether they were ever relieved, I am unable to say.

The next day we walked four or five miles to Placentia. We who were prisoners were deposited in our old station, the guardhouse. Mr. Baggs got his discharge, and the crew was sent in shallops to St. John's.

EIGHT

I Was a Prisoner of War

About one month later, the end of October, the *Fairy*, a sloop of war of eighteen guns, came into the harbor to convoy a few merchantmen to St. John's. The merchantmen, bound for Lisbon, Portugal, were short of hands, and Mr. Loyd, Babb, and Annis were put on board them. They were promised their liberty in Lisbon. Whether they ever found their way to their native shores, I cannot say.

Willis and I were put on board the *Fairy* to be conveyed to St. John's. This sloop of war was commanded by Captain Yeo, a complete tyrant, and I now feared my fate was to serve his majesty on board a man-of-war the rest of my days, a service I detested.

Willis and I were called upon the quarter-deck. Captain Yeo asked us a few questions and then turned to his officers and said, "They are a couple of fine lads for his majesty's service. See that they do their duty, one in the *foretop* and the other in the *maintop*."

Willis replied that he was afraid to go up so high. He said he was subject to fits, and he was afraid he should fall down and kill himself.

I said that I was a prisoner of war. I could not consent to serve against my country.

With very hard words and several threats, we were ordered off the quarter-deck and commanded to do our duty in the *waist*. The tops were much more honorable stations than the waist, but we were determined not to serve his majesty in either position. We therefore left the quarter-deck in haste and went below into the prisoners' station.

In a day or two, all hands were called on deck. This is performed with a certain ceremony. The boatswain's mate stands at the fore hatchway, and he blows a loud and long blast with his pipe. He then halloos out, "All hands, ahoy!" He performs the same ceremony at the main hatchway and the after hatchway. After suitable time is given for the men to get on deck, the mate goes down to see if there are any skulkers.

On this occasion, he found Willis and me below. He began to rave at us, and hastening toward us, he commanded us on deck. We informed him that we were prisoners of war.

"Tell me nothing about prisoners," said he. "Upon deck immediately!"

We still kept our stations. He then began a most furious attack upon us with his *rattan*. For a while, we sternly adhered to our purpose while he alternately thrashed one, then the other. We should have resisted, but we were afraid of the consequences. He became more and more enraged

and determined to conquer, and we thought it best to clear out. We mounted the deck with him at our heels, repeating his strokes.

The carpenter and boatswain each had a berth, a small room, forward of the fore hatchway. The carpenter, whose name was Fox, was sitting in his berth and looking on while the boatswain's mate was whipping us.

The thought of serving his majesty on board a man-of-war was so painful to me, I directly left the deck and went below. I could not endure the thought of being deprived of liberty and spending my days on board an enemy's ship.

Mr. Fox was still sitting in his cabin when I went below.

He called to me and asked me to come to his room. I went in, and he kindly asked me to sit down, which I did. He then said, "I see, my lad, that you are obliged to do duty."

"Yes, sir," said I, "but very much against my inclination."

Said he, "It is wrong, but it would not do for me to interfere. However, I was thinking to do you a favor. His majesty allows me two helpers, but I have none. If you will take a little care here, I will excuse you from keeping watch and all other duty."

I hesitated, fearing to perform any voluntary service. I was afraid it should prove unfavorable to me.

Mr. Fox noticed that I was in suspense about the matter and said, "You need not fear that this will be unfavorable to you, and you will be much less exposed if you work for me than you will be if you have to do your duty before the mast. It is in vain for you to think to escape that, for Captain Yeo is a very arbitrary man. He is not liked by the crew, and his officers do not set much by him. I intend to leave the ship when we get home. You may be assured that I will be your friend."

He was so kind, I put my confidence in him, and it was not misplaced. He proved to be a faithful friend.

The boatswain and gunner ate with Mr. Fox. Each had a boy, so my service was very light.

Within a day or two after this, the ship arrived at St. John's. I soon ascertained that the cartel had sailed for Boston several weeks before, and there were no longer any prisoners on the prison ship. I was appalled, although I had little ground to expect that the cartel would have waited until we arrived. We were now destined to see old England.

We had a short, but rather rough, passage to England. Willis and I were called to quarters several times, but it so happened that neither of us was given any assignment. Whether we were overlooked or whether this was a plan by the officers, I am unable to say. At any rate, we thought it a very fortunate circumstance on our part.

We arrived at Plymouth, England, in November, 1781. I must confess that I felt a certain kind of reverence and solemnity that I cannot well describe when I saw the land of my forefathers. Yet when reflecting upon my situation and the haughtiness of the king and the government's injustice and cruelty to its children, I felt an indignant, if not a revengeful, spirit.

Mr. Fox proposed to adopt me as his son if I could not get released from the ship. He had a wife in Bristol, but no child. He said that he did not intend to follow the sea, and he could, if he pleased, quit the ship and work in his majesty's shipyard.

I expressed my gratitude for his kindness, but I informed him that it was my design to use every endeavor to get to America again. He did not blame me, and he told me that if he could see any opportunity in my favor, he would apprise me of it.

There was now some prospect of Captain Yeo's being removed from the command of the ship. In the meantime, she was preparing for sea again.

The men, especially the officers, lived high while the ship was in port. In our *mess*, we had plenty of fresh beef, mutton, fowls, and vegetables. This was very acceptable to me after having been without every kind of vegetable and fresh provision except fish for seven or eight months.

We had been in port several weeks when Captain Yeo took his leave of the ship without any ceremony or respect being shown him from the crew. Shortly after, the new captain came on board, and he was saluted with three cheers.

A day or two later, Mr. Fox came into his cabin where I was and said to me, "Sherburne, the captain is walking alone on the quarter-deck. I think it is a good time for you to go and speak to him. It may be that he will consider you a prisoner of war."

I trembled with fear. If I should fail in this, my fate would be sealed unless Mr. Fox would take me with him, and even then, I must be a British subject. There was no time to lose, and I informed Willis of my plan and requested him to accompany me. He readily consented, and we walked to the quarter-deck where we met the captain as he was walking forward.

"What is your wish, my lads?" said he.

I replied, "We are American prisoners, sir, taken off the coast of Newfoundland. We were put on board the *Duchess of Cumberland* to go to St. John's, expecting to be sent from thence to Boston to be exchanged. The ship was lost on Cape St. Mary's, and we were taken to Placentia and there put on board this ship. It is our wish, sir, to be considered prisoners of war and to go to prison."

Said he, "You may go forward, my lads, and I will inquire into your cause."

We bowed and retired. Mr. Fox anxiously waited our return.

In about half an hour, word was given out from the captain that Sherburne and Willis were to get ready to go into the transport boat. We felt ready to leap for joy. We were to have the honor and privilege of going to prison. I saw tears in Mr. Fox's eyes, and I am certain that some ran down my cheeks freely. He gave me some shirts and stockings and his best wishes. So we parted.

NINE

Committed to Mill Prison

We left the *Fairy* in Plymouth Sound and shaped our course for the *Dunkirk*, the harbor's guard ship. All prisoners brought into port are put on board this vessel, as are all men who are impressed in and about this port.

There were no American prisoners on the *Dunkirk* when we arrived, only impressed men, and more of them were brought on board by press gangs nearly every night. The *Dunkirk* sometimes had five or six gangs out at the same time. They consisted of six, eight, or ten unprincipled, sturdy fellows, and it was not uncommon for those who were impressed to be brought on board shockingly bruised and mangled.

A few days after we went on board, a dozen prisoners were brought to the ship and shortly after, a few more. The prisoners first brought on board were sent ashore a few days later to pass an examination before the judges of the admiralty, and I was surprised that those prisoners should precede us.

The day after, the others were called and sent ashore. Willis and I now began to feel alarmed, for we had understood that prisoners were sent ashore in rotation, as they came on board. We feared that we should be turned off to the first ship which might want hands. We asked the ship's clerk why we were not sent in our turn. The clerk inquired what vessel's crew we came from and what our names were. We informed him, but he knew nothing about us. However, the clerk promised to make diligent search for our names.

Eleven more prisoners were brought on board, and when the time came to send them ashore, our names were called as well. Whether our list had been mislaid and had now come to light, or whether the clerk sent on board the *Fairy* for a new one, I never inquired.

Thirteen prisoners were ordered on board the boat and were landed at Plymouth Dock. We were escorted from the wharf to the court of admiralty and conducted into a room by ourselves. And here we waited a while in awful suspense. We had one more trying scene to endure. The judges in their examinations were careful to select all Englishmen and Irishmen for his majesty's service. Sometimes they challenged Americans, insisted that they were British subjects, and sent them on board one of his majesty's ships of war.

We had to pass an examination individually, and I was called in first before the judges. They were elderly gentlemen, and all wore large white wigs. There were also several other persons present. The judges asked me many questions about where I served and how I came to be in England. I was then conducted back to the rest of my ship-mates, and Willis was questioned.

After all had been examined, I was called in before the judges a second time, and most of the questions were asked me again. This alarmed me, and I feared that they were laying a snare for me. One of the judges asked a gentleman, who was sitting in another part of the room, if my state-ments agreed with what I had said before. He answered in the affirmative.

The other twelve were then called in and one of the judges pronounced the sentence. "You are severally and in-dividually committed to Mill Prison for rebellion, piracy, and high treason on his majesty's high seas, there to remain at his majesty's pleasure until he sees fit to pardon or other-wise dispose of you."

We were then led to a door where soldiers were waiting to conduct us to the prison, a walk of about a mile and a half. It was a peculiar gratification to think of entering Mill Prison, and I felt a high degree of animation.

At length, we came to the outer gate which, groaning on its hinges, opened to receive us into the outer yard. The commissary's office and the cook room made two sides of this yard. It was separated from the prison yard by a strong wooden gate. In this yard, a sentinel stood continually, and a woman, known as "Aunt Anna," sold supplies, bread, butter, tobacco, needles, thread, and every other article for which prisoners might call, from her handcart.

As the inner gate opened, we heard an outcry from within. "More prisoners! More prisoners!" We were urged forward into the yard by soldiers with fixed bayonets, and we saw prisoners rushing towards the gate from all directions to see if any of their acquaintances were to be found amongst the newcomers.

Before I could look about, I was greeted by a prisoner who seized my hand and said, "How fare ye, shipmate? Where are you from?"

I told him I hailed from Piscataqua, the name of the river dividing Maine from New Hampshire. The Piscataqua men were then called, and they formed a circle round me, I being the only one who came from that river. There were seven men from Portsmouth and at least ten from nearby Kittery. Mr. Tibbits was the only person amongst them with whom I had had any acquaintance, though most of the Portsmouth people had known my father.

It was now near night. I had eaten nothing since the morning, and I had got to a hungry place. One of the men bought me a penny roll and a half penny worth of butter, which was very acceptable.

Within the prison, the men had their own government, and they made many decisions regarding daily life. The next day, my friends held a consultation amongst themselves respecting me. One of them said, "It would be a pity if this young countryman should spend his time as many of the boys do, gaming. He is fatherless, and he has no education. Perhaps he might be persuaded to go to school."

"If he will," said one prisoner, "I will give him some paper."

"I will give him some quills and ink," said another.

"And I will undertake to instruct him," said Mr. Tibbits.

The men then appointed a committee to confer with me

upon the subject. I promised to deny myself and adhere to their advice.

Although I had never had six months' schooling in my life, I could read tolerably well. However, I could not write my name or enumerate three figures.

I commenced writing with Mr. Tibbits and made rapid progress. My mind was entirely taken up with the business, and my friends were much gratified with my improvement. I soon became entirely indifferent to all kinds of gaming and found sufficient amusement with my pen and pencil. When I required some relaxation from my studies, it was more agreeable to me to walk alone in the yard than to join in any kind of play.

Mill Prison had three buildings, and a space near them answered as a yard. On the south end, there was a stone wall which was fourteen feet high and topped with broken bottles set in mortar to prevent anyone from climbing over. There was a similar wall on the east. By day, there were two sentinels in the yard, and at night, there were at least four guards in the area and as large a number without the walls.

There had been no release or exchange of prisoners from this place since the beginning of the war, and I think the number of American prisoners was between 800 and 1,000. Some had been there nearly seven years. A few had tired of prison and shipped on board his majesty's ships and thereby were absolved from the crimes of rebellion, treason, and piracy.

The provision while I was there was, in general, pretty good, but we had not half enough of it. I think we were allowed twelve ounces of bread, twelve ounces of beef, and some broth per day. At eleven o'clock, we drew our food. Some would eat all their allowance as fast as it came, others made two or three parts of it.

Benjamin Franklin took a deep interest in the prisoners in England, and he tried to furnish each prisoner with a shilling a week. It was very difficult for him to obtain funds, and sometimes this donation would stop for weeks or even months. After I had been in prison a month, I received my first donation, and I found that it added much to my comfort. It served to supply me with a comfortable meal each day.

There was nothing left undone to obtain a little money in order to augment our small stock of provisions. Some of the Kittery people had money with them when they were taken. These men furnished themselves with a kettle, a few pounds of coffee, and using meat bones for fuel, they made coffee and sold a pint of it for half a penny.

Miniature ship-building was the most extensive business which was carried on. Sloops of war, frigates, two-deckers, and even three-deckers were built here and sold to local boys whose curiosity led them to take a peep at the Yankees.

One man from Salem exceeded all others in this business. He built a three-decker and rigged her completely. She was between three and four feet in length and showed three tiers of guns. By pulling gently on a cable, he could make the guns move in their portholes. He was twenty-two months in building her.

Every evening, the officers on guard came into the yard and gave orders for every man to go into his building. An officer stood at the front door and counted the men as they entered. The doors were then locked. In the morning, the men were counted again as they left the building.

There was one regiment which the prisoners were very much against. When a prisoner managed to escape, it was an object with the rest to conceal it until the prisoner was far away and this hated regiment mounted guard, so it would be blamed for the escape.

There were a number of boys in the prison and dependence was placed on those lads to make up the number of escaped men. In the morning, prisoners first out the front door stationed themselves in front of the side yard's gate, which had a hole designed to pass cans of water through, about four feet from the ground. The hole was not large enough for a man to get through, but small boys could do so with help. After a boy had been counted out, some prisoners took him up and crowded him through the hole to prisoners on the other side. The boy then entered the building's side door and presented himself to be numbered again. Sometimes the lads had to do this a second or third time, depending upon how many men had escaped. In the evening, the process was reversed, and boys were counted several times as they entered and re-entered the building.

At length, the hated regiment came on guard, and there was no more squeezing boys through the hole. When it was fully ascertained that men were missing, there was no small stir among the soldiers.

I diligently pursued my studies of arithmetic and geometry with a design to learn navigation, but when spring came, there were many sick prisoners amongst us. Several of my townsmen were quite unwell. They had been very kind to me, and I cheerfully devoted myself to their service.

75

One morning when I rose up in my hammock, my head ached violently. I thought I would lie down a few minutes and then get up and attend to my sick friends. I rose up again, but my sight left me. I was soon surrounded by my neighbors, and I recollect hearing some of them say, "Sherburne is out of his head." The physicians, at this time, visited the prison every day, and one of them was called to look at me. He ordered me to the hospital.

I was almost entirely deranged for several weeks. When my reason returned, I discovered that I was exceedingly weak, and when I began to mend, I did so very slowly.

TEN

Joy Indescribable

In spring, the prisoners received the intelligence that shortly there was to be a general exchange of prisoners, and about the time I got upon my legs again, the *Lady's Adventure* had actually got into the Sound. There was joy indescribable among the prisoners. My doctor, in order to raise my spirits, told me the ship had arrived to take us to our own country. She would sail in two or three weeks, and he said that I must take the best possible care of myself so that I might go in her.

Finally, the time arrived for the doctor to discharge from the hospital all who were recovered. Every man went to his own bed and sat until the doctor passed him. He examined me with some pleasant ceremony, but I perceived that he had not taken down my name, which meant I was not to be released. My heart almost sank within me. I arose and followed him, and as he was about to leave the hospital, I said, "Doctor, I believe you have not got my name."

He replied, "God bless you my son. It will never do for you to think of leaving the hospital in your situation. You are a more suitable person to enter a hospital than to leave one."

"Sir," said I, "you promised me that I should go in this ship."

Said he, "I was in hopes you would have been able to go in her, but you are so sick that it will never do. You would not live. There are 400 or more going, and they will be so crowded, you will die directly. We have had such a hard time in raising you so far that I should be very sorry to lose you now, especially through imprudence. There is another ship going in a week or two. Have patience and stay until she is ready to go."

"But, sir, all my acquaintances and townsmen are going in this ship, and she is going near my home. I have a number of good friends who will take good care of me. But if they all go and leave me, I shall never get home."

Lawrence, the hospital's kind overseer and a prisoner of war, and twenty others were listening to the doctor and me, and as I turned my eyes toward Lawrence, I saw tears trickling down his manly face. The beloved doctor was in the same condition, and my readers must judge for themselves how it was with me.

Lawrence then said, "Doctor, I don't know but that you may as well discharge Sherburne. I am going home in the same ship, and if you will release him, I will give you my word that I will pay particular attention to him."

"Well, well," said the doctor. "In that case, Lawrence, I will discharge him, for I can trust him in your care. But if he dies, his blood must be upon his own head."

"Oh, sir," said I, feeling almost well, "the sea always agrees with me, and I believe I should gain faster on board the ship than I should here."

The good doctor placed my name on the list of the discharged. That day we were guarded from the hospital to the prison.

The time finally came for us to embark for our native land, and the people generally were all life on the occasion. Some of them had been in prison more than six years.

I walked poorly even with two canes. With difficulty, I got to the water, about twenty rods, but I was unable to get on board the boat without help. When we got alongside of the ship, my Portsmouth and Kittery friends put me on board, and they released Lawrence from his charge.

I believe the ship did not lie in port many hours after we got on board before we were under weigh for the land of liberty. My friends took care of me, and I gained very fast. In the course of a week, I was able to wait on the mess. This was only to boil the teakettle night and morning. In a *fortnight*, I was able to get to the masthead.

We had not been out many days before there was a revolution on board. His majesty granted us only two-thirds allowance, but it was ascertained that there was enough food on board for full allowance. We were determined to have enough to eat. A number of officers among us laid the plan. At a certain signal, we were to rush upon the quarterdeck and take the helm, and our officers were to inform the captain that they had command of his ship. When this happened, the ship's crew and officers made no resistance. They were under forty, and there were 400 of us. All that we requested was full allowance, and having obtained our purpose, the ship was given up to the captain again.

We had a long but pleasant passage. The ship was ordered to Boston, but it fell in to the east of that port. There were many Marblehead, Massachusetts, men on board, and they insisted upon going into Marblehead, and of course, all to the east of that port landed there, myself and Willis among the rest. Thus we once more set our feet on the American shore.

I recollected that by Captain Willis's recommendation, the crew of the *Greyhound* had appointed Mr. Foster of nearby Salem to be our agent. I inquired about the gentleman and found his office. Mr. Foster knew nothing of us personally, though our names had been given to him as belonging to the crew. When in conversation with Mr. Foster, Captain Tucker, the man who had been the first lieutenant of the *Greyhound*, came in. (It is probable that Mr. Foster sent for him.)

We learned from Captain Tucker that nothing was known of our fate since we left the privateer. It was supposed that we were lost at sea. We also learned that the *Greyhound* had taken a valuable prize after we left her and that the prize got safely into Salem. Later, the *Greyhound* was captured and taken into Halifax. The crew, after a short confinement, was exchanged, and all got home.

Mr. Foster informed us that our share of the prize was sixty-three pounds *sterling* each. I had left power of attorney with my mother to draw my share of the goods, and Willis's father had drawn his share. Consequently, there was noth-

ing coming to us. However, Captain Tucker and Mr. Foster
had the goodness to give us two or three dollars each to
bear our expenses home.

We took leave of our generous friends and started our
journey with a pleasure not easily described. We had been
companions in our travels for about a year and a quarter,
and we had always been in perfect harmony and friendship.
We now had about forty-five miles further to journey with
each other, and having no other company, we discussed the
trying scenes we had passed together and the joys we shortly
expected in meeting our friends.

My mother, brothers, and sisters had despaired of ever seeing me again until some of my shipmates, who were ahead of me, gave information of my being on the way home. I was, nevertheless, to them, almost as one who rose from the dead.

Willis tarried a night with me. In the morning I accompanied him to the wharf where he found a coaster going to Saco, which was within four miles of Cape Porpoise where he lived. He went on board, and there we parted. We never met again.

I was, at this time, blessed with good health and felt as though I had never been otherwise. It was now unspeakably pleasant to visit my uncles, aunts, and cousins. It seemed as if nothing could be more entertaining to them than to hear my stories about a shipwreck, a British man-of-war, and imprisonment.

AFTERWORD

Shortly after Andrew Sherburne returned to Portsmouth in 1782, he decided to go back to sea to earn a living. He joined the crew of the *Scorpion*, which was under the command of Captain Tibbits, the man who had been Andrew's tutor in Mill Prison. The *Scorpion* was captured by a British man-of-war, and Andrew and thirteen others were taken prisoner.

Although fighting on land in the colonies was over at this time, peace treaties had not been signed or ratified, and some British sea captains continued to capture Americans. The British held some of their prisoners on ships in New York harbor, one of two cities the English still occupied.

Andrew was put aboard the *Jersey* where the living conditions were horrible. He wrote, "The ship was extremely filthy and abounded with vermin [and] crowded; many of the men were very low spirited. . . . Our provisions . . . consisted of worm eaten ship bread and salt beef. It was supposed that this bread and beef had been condemned in the British navy. The bread had been so eaten by weevils, one might easily crush it in the hand and blow it away."

Contaminated food and water, plus filth, made many prisoners ill. The worst cases were moved to a hospital ship; the rest lived side by side with other prisoners on the *Jersey*, including many with smallpox. Andrew fell sick in January, 1783. At times, he was mentally deranged, possibly due to a high fever, and he was finally taken to the hospital ship.

Conditions aboard the hospital ship were even worse than those on the *Jersey*. The vessel was so overcrowded, two patients were assigned to every bunk. Andrew's partner was seriously ill, and as Andrew said, "running down very fast." Sherburne awoke one morning to find his partner dead. When he asked the nurses to remove the body, they did not do so for nearly half an hour. Death was so common, Andrew reported seeing corpses piled in the lower hatchway, waiting to be taken away.

The sick were fed poorly, and they lacked enough blankets and clothing to keep them warm. During the last part of January, it was so cold on the ship Andrew spent much of his time and energy rubbing his feet and legs to keep them from freezing.

Unlikely as it seems, he managed to recover enough aboard the hospital ship to be returned to the *Jersey*. However, he never recovered fully from the ordeal, and at age seventeen, he faced a future full of health problems. His left leg was permanently damaged due to the cold temperatures he endured, and his circulation was poor. He would never enjoy good health again. Andrew remained aboard the *Jersey* until the peace treaties were ratified, and the British withdrew from New York.

After Andrew's release in 1783, he rejoined Captain Tibbits for a voyage to Lisbon, Portugal. Sherburne found the work difficult due to his poor health, and he was forced to find another way to make a living.

One of Andrew's uncles who had served on the *Ranger* with him, James Weymouth, persuaded Sherburne to try teaching. His uncle knew that Andrew had been tutored well, and Weymouth was sure he could help his nephew get a position in Cornish, Maine, the site of Weymouth's new home. Andrew agreed to try this, and he moved to Cornish in 1786. Now twenty years old, he taught in a small school, and he was well-liked by his students.

But most teaching positions then were only a few months long in rural communities. Children had to help with farm work, especially during planting and harvesting seasons which were much longer than they are today, since few labor-saving devices were available at that time. Students attended school only when they weren't needed at home, and the school year was organized around the farming calendar. As a result, teachers only worked part of the year, and they were paid accordingly.

Because the pay was poor, Andrew had to find additional work to support himself. He enjoyed mathematics, and he decided to take up surveying after finding someone who could tutor him. He learned quickly, and his skills were in great demand in and around Cornish as newcomers plotted their land or old-timers expanded their farms.

Over the years, Andrew became more and more interested in religion. He listened to local preachers whenever he could, studied the Bible, and talked about faith and God with his friends. Eventually, he became a Baptist minister, and he served as a chaplain for some of the American troops in the war against England in 1812.

Andrew married twice. His first wife, Jane Muchamore, died in 1815. They had two children, John and Betsy. Andrew's second wife was Betsy Miller. They had four children, Andrew, Samuel, Mary Jane, and Eliza Ann.

Like many other men at the time, Sherburne wanted to move west. Shortly after his second marriage, he found work as a missionary and a teacher, first in western New York and later in Ohio. These positions paid poorly, and Andrew often had serious financial difficulties.

In 1827, he moved back to New York State. It is here, at age 62, that he began his memoirs.

GLOSSARY

Allowance. The normal supply of food and drink given to a sailor. When a voyage was longer than expected and food-stuffs could run out, the allowance might be cut in half, or only some portion given. A lowered ration was also used to punish a rebellious crew.

Apothecary. A druggist or pharmacist.

Ballast. Any heavy material carried low in a boat or ship to give the vessel stability on water.

Bank. A long, broad elevation rising from an ocean floor. Above the bank, water is shallow and fish are often abundant. Grand Bank, off the coast of Newfoundland, is one of the longest banks, about 300 miles in length.

Battery. A fortification equipped with mounted guns.

Boatswain. An officer on a ship in charge of riggings, anchors, and cables.

Brig. A two-masted ship with square sails on both masts.

Broadside. A volley of cannon shot fired to hit the whole side of a ship above the water line.

Cartel. A group of ships acting as one, having one purpose; for example, a group of ships taking prisoners to America for a prisoner exchange.

Coaster. A ship that trades along a seacoast.

Colonial Congress. The Continental Congress, made up of representatives from each colony, governed the colonies during the Revolutionary War.

Colors. Flags and banners.

Commissary. An officer in charge of supplying food and equipment to service men and prisoners of war.

Consort. One ship traveling with another.

Convoy. To accompany or escort something to protect it.

Foretop. A platform at the top of the foremast.

Fortnight. A British term meaning two weeks.

Frigate. A war vessel designed for high speed, often used for scouting the enemy.

Gulf Stream. A warm ocean current that flows from the Gulf of Mexico northward along the coast of the United States.

League. A British measurement roughly equal to three miles.

Leeward. The direction opposite the wind's source.

Letters of marque and reprisal. Documents issued by the Continental Congress, or in some cases, by individual colonies, that gave sailors permission to seize enemy ships. Men who held letters were called privateers.

Lines. A distribution or arrangement of armed ships in a convoy to protect merchant ships from the enemy. Although a line could take many shapes, it usually circled the ships being protected.

Logwood. A brownish-red wood from the West Indies used to make a dye.

Maintop. A platform at the top of the mainmast.

Masthead. The highest point on a mast.

Mess. A group that eats together.

Parole. Parole allowed prisoners of war to move about freely in a particular area, a city, for example. It was usually granted only to officers and their boys in the Revolutionary War and then only after officers promised they would not bear arms against their captors.

Rattan. A stick or switch made from the stems of palms.

Redoubt. A large mound of earth made to reinforce a fort or fixed position in battle.

Reef. To roll or tie back part of a sail to cut down on the amount of wind hitting it, thereby lowering a ship's speed.

Rod. A measurement equal to sixteen and one-half feet.

Rudder. The part of a ship's steering mechanism that is located under water at the ship's stern.

Schooner. A sailing vessel with two or more masts, a foremast and a taller mainmast.

Shallop. A small boat, usually used for fishing.

Shrouds. A set of strong ropes that run from the masthead to the sides of a ship to help support the mast.

Skiff. A small boat that can be rowed by one person.

Sloops of war. Ships mounting guns on only one deck.

Specie. Coined money. During the Revolutionary War, coins had more value than did paper money. When the Continental Congress needed money to pay for the war, it simply issued more paper dollars, which were easy to print. Eventually there were so many of them, they had little value.

Squadron. Ships assigned to a special duty, for instance, escorting merchant ships.

Stamp Act. An act of the British crown that required colonists to affix stamps to many different goods, including newspapers, pamphlets, playing cards, and all legal documents, to show that a tax had been paid on them.

Staterooms. Small rooms on a ship, sometimes occupied by officers.

Sterling. A pound sterling, or pound, was the standard unit of British currency.

Struck. To strike a ship's colors is a sign of surrender.

Waist. The central part of a ship, the deck area between the forecastle and the quarter-deck.

Warp. To move a ship from one place to another by hauling it on a warp, a line or a rope.

Western Islands. The Hebrides, a group of islands located off the west coast of Scotland.

Windward. The direction toward the wind source.

FOR MORE INFORMATION

A number of books have been written about colonial sailors, some of which were used as reference material for the introduction to this book. For more information on the Continental navy and its enemy, the British fleet, read Trevor Nevitt Dupuy's book, *The Military History of Revolutionary War Naval Battles* (New York: Franklin Watts, 1970), or *The American Heritage History of Seafaring America* written by Alexander Kinnan Laing (New York: American Heritage Publishing Co., Inc., 1974). *Men-of-War*, by David Howarth (Alexandria, Va.: Time-Life Books, 1978), has lots of information about press gangs and the British navy, and Howard I. Chapelle's book, *The History of the American Sailing Navy* (New York: W. W. Norton and Co., 1949), examines everyday life aboard a ship. Both will help readers better understand what it was like to sail in fighting vessels.

There are also some interesting books on privateers. One of the oldest is Edgar Stanton Maclay's book, *A History of American Privateers* (New York: D. Appleton and Co., 1899). His text gives information about battles and a daring escape from Mill Prison. *The American Privateers*, by Donald Barr Chidsey (New York: Dodd, Mead and Co., 1962), covers privateering in the Revolutionary War, the War of 1812, and the Civil War, when the practice was finally outlawed. A more recent book about privateers is *Privateers of Seventy-Six* (Indianapolis: Bobbs-Merrill, 1976) written by Fred J. Cook. It discusses some of the sailors' most daring escapades.

One of the naval heroes of the war was John Paul Jones. Most libraries carry several biographies about him. Samuel Eliot Morison's book, *John Paul Jones, a Sailor's Biography* (Boston: Little, Brown, and Co., 1959) is probably the best known and most detailed. It has a chapter about the *Ranger*, Andrew's first ship, which was once under Jones's command.

And finally, for more first-hand accounts of events in the Revolutionary War, read some of the episodes in *The Spirit of 'Seventy-Six* (Indianapolis: Bobbs-Merrill Co., Inc., 1958), two volumes of eyewitness accounts edited by Henry Steele Commager and Richard B. Morris. The second volume contains some vivid descriptions of the prison ship the *Jersey*, part of the debate in the Continental Congress over starting a navy, and sailors' accounts of some important naval battles.